THE ESSENTIAL ISTANBUL TRAVEL GUIDE 2023 & BEYOND

Must-See Attractions,foodie,nightlife and Experiences for First-Time Visitors

Rosa R. Coleman

Table of content

- Description of the most popular and unique bars in the city
- Recommended drinks and menu items
- Location, atmosphere, and dress code information
- Average cost of a drink

Introduction to Istanbul: An Overview of the City's History, Culture, and Geography

Istanbul is a city that is both ancient and modern, straddling the divide between Europe and Asia, and filled with a rich and complex history that spans over 2,000 years. As the largest city in Turkey and the fifth-largest city in the world, Istanbul is a vibrant and bustling metropolis that offers visitors a unique blend of cultures, religions, and traditions.

The history of Istanbul can be traced back to the 7th century BC when it was founded as Byzantium by the Greeks. Over the centuries, the city was ruled by various empires, including the Roman, Byzantine, and Ottoman Empires, each leaving their mark on the city's architecture, art, and culture.

Istanbul has also been an important center of trade and commerce, connecting Europe and Asia through its strategic location on the Bosphorus Strait.

Today, Istanbul is a cosmopolitan city that boasts a diverse population of over 15 million people, including Muslims, Christians, and Jews, and is home to some of the most iconic landmarks and attractions in the world. The city is divided into two distinct parts: the European side and the Asian side, which are separated by the Bosphorus Strait.

The European side of Istanbul is the more popular and touristy side, home to the city's historic core and most famous attractions, such as the Blue Mosque, Hagia Sophia, and the Grand Bazaar. The Asian side, on the other hand, is a more laid-back and residential area that is known for its trendy cafes, shops, and bars.

Istanbul's culture is as diverse and eclectic as its history. The city is a melting pot of different traditions and influences, with a rich culinary scene that blends Turkish, Greek, and Middle Eastern flavors. Istanbul is also home to a vibrant arts and music scene, with numerous galleries, theaters, and performance venues throughout the city.

The geography of Istanbul is as unique as its culture and history. The city is located on two continents, Europe and Asia, and is surrounded by water on three sides. The Bosphorus Strait runs through the heart of the city, dividing it into two distinct parts, and is home to some of the most beautiful views and sunsets in the world.

Overall, Istanbul is a city that offers visitors a truly unique and unforgettable experience. With its rich history, vibrant culture, and stunning geography, there is no other city in the world quite like it.

Istanbul is a city that has played a significant role in world history, and has been at the center of many significant events. Throughout its history, the city has been a place of political, economic, and cultural importance, and has been the site of many conquests, battles, and revolutions. Its strategic location has made it a target of many invaders throughout the centuries, but it has always managed to bounce back and thrive.

In addition to its rich history and culture, Istanbul is a city of incredible natural beauty. The Bosphorus Strait, which runs through the heart of the city, is one of the most breathtaking waterways in the world, offering visitors stunning views of the city's skyline and surroundings. Istanbul is also home to many parks and green spaces, such as the Emirgan Park and the Yildiz Park, which offer a tranquil escape from the bustling city.

Istanbul's cuisine is another aspect of the city that is renowned throughout the world. Turkish food is known for its rich flavors and variety, and Istanbul is the perfect place to sample some of the country's most famous dishes. From the savory kebabs and grilled meats to the sweet baklava and Turkish delight, Istanbul's culinary scene is sure to delight any food lover.

The architecture of Istanbul is also a testament to the city's rich history and cultural influences. The city is home to some of the most iconic and impressive buildings in the world, including the Blue Mosque, Hagia Sophia, and the Topkapi Palace. These buildings are a reflection of the city's past, and offer visitors a glimpse into the lives and traditions of the people who lived in Istanbul over the centuries.

In recent years, Istanbul has also emerged as a hub for innovation and entrepreneurship. The city has a thriving startup scene, and has been recognized as one of the top startup cities in the world. This has attracted a new generation of entrepreneurs and investors to the city, and has helped to create a culture of innovation and creativity.

Overall, Istanbul is a city that offers something for everyone, whether you're a history buff, a foodie, a nature lover, or a tech enthusiast. Its rich history, vibrant culture, and stunning geography make it a truly unique and unforgettable destination, and a must-visit for anyone traveling to Turkey or the surrounding region.

Planning Your Trip to Istanbul: Practical Tips and Information for First-Time Visitors

Planning a trip to Istanbul can be an exciting and overwhelming experience, especially if it's your first time visiting the city. Istanbul is a large and bustling city, filled with many attractions and hidden gems, and it's important to plan your trip carefully to make the most of your time there. Here are some practical tips and information to help you plan your trip to Istanbul:

- Best time to visit: The best time to visit Istanbul is from April to June and from September to November, when the weather is mild and the crowds are smaller. The summer months can be hot and crowded, while the winter months can be chilly and rainy.

- Getting there: Istanbul is served by two airports - Atatürk Airport on the European side and Sabiha Gökçen Airport on the Asian side. Both airports are well-connected to the city center by public transportation, including metro, bus, and taxi.

- Visa requirements: Visitors to Turkey may require a visa, depending on their country of origin. Visitors from most countries can obtain an e-visa online before their trip, or obtain a visa on arrival at the airport.

- Accommodation: Istanbul offers a wide range of accommodation options, from budget hostels to luxury hotels. The most popular areas to stay in Istanbul are Sultanahmet and Taksim, both located on the European side of the city.

- Getting around: Istanbul is a large city, and the best way to get around is by using a combination of public transportation and walking. The city has an extensive public transportation system, including metro, tram, bus, and ferry.

- Safety: Istanbul is a safe city, but like any large city, visitors should take precautions to avoid pickpockets and scams. It's also a good idea to avoid the more remote and less well-lit areas of the city, especially at night.

- Currency: The official currency of Turkey is the Turkish lira. Most shops and restaurants in Istanbul accept credit cards, but it's a good idea to have some cash on hand for small purchases.

- Language: Turkish is the official language of Turkey, but many people in Istanbul also speak English. Learning a few basic Turkish phrases can be helpful, especially when interacting with locals.

- Must-see attractions: Istanbul is home to many iconic landmarks and attractions, such as the Blue Mosque, Hagia Sophia, Topkapi Palace, and the Grand Bazaar. It's a good idea to prioritize your must-see attractions and plan your itinerary accordingly.

- Food and drink: Turkish cuisine is known for its rich flavors and variety, and Istanbul is the perfect place to sample some of the country's most famous dishes, such as kebabs, baklava, and Turkish tea. It's also a good idea to try some of the local street food, such as simit and börek.

- Dress code: Istanbul is a modern and cosmopolitan city, but it's still important to dress modestly, especially when visiting religious sites. It's a good idea to dress in layers, as the weather can be unpredictable.

- Culture and customs: Istanbul has a rich and complex culture, with influences from both the East and West. It's important to respect local customs and traditions, such as removing your shoes when entering a mosque, and avoiding public displays of affection.

- Shopping: Istanbul is home to many traditional bazaars and markets, such as the Grand Bazaar, the Spice Bazaar, and the Çukurcuma Antiques Market. These markets offer a unique shopping experience, where you can find everything from spices and sweets to handcrafted goods and antiques.

- Festivals and events: Istanbul hosts many cultural and artistic events throughout the year, such as the Istanbul International Film Festival, the Istanbul Jazz Festival, and the Istanbul Biennial. It's a good idea to check the event calendar before your trip, as these events can be a great way to experience the city's vibrant cultural scene.

- Day trips: Istanbul is surrounded by many scenic and historic destinations that make for great day trips, such as the Princes' Islands, the city of Edirne, and the ancient city of Troy. It's a good idea to plan these day trips in advance, as transportation and logistics can be challenging.

- Health and medical care: Istanbul has a good healthcare system, with many public and private hospitals and clinics. It's a good idea to purchase travel insurance before your trip, and to research the nearest medical facilities in case of an emergency.

- Internet and communication: Istanbul has a good internet infrastructure, with many free public Wi-Fi hotspots available throughout the city. It's also a good idea to purchase a local SIM card to stay connected on the go.

- Photography: Istanbul is a photographer's paradise, with many beautiful landmarks and scenic views to capture. However, it's important to be respectful of local customs and avoid taking photographs in sensitive areas, such as inside mosques or of military personnel.

- Sustainability: Istanbul is a city that faces many environmental and sustainability challenges, such as air pollution and waste management. It's a good idea to be mindful of your environmental impact, and to support local businesses and initiatives that promote sustainability.

- Local experiences: One of the best ways to experience Istanbul is by immersing yourself in the local culture and way of life. This could include taking a cooking class, visiting a local hamam, or attending a traditional Turkish music concert. By engaging with the local community, you can gain a deeper understanding and appreciation of Istanbul's rich culture and history.

By following these practical tips and information, you can ensure that your trip to Istanbul is a smooth and enjoyable experience. With its rich history, vibrant culture, and stunning geography, Istanbul is a city that is sure to leave a lasting impression on any visitor.

Sultanahmet Square: Exploring the Heart of Old Istanbul

Sultanahmet Square, also known as the Hippodrome, is a historic public space located in the heart of Istanbul's Old City. Surrounded by some of Istanbul's most iconic landmarks, including the Hagia Sophia, the Blue Mosque, and the Basilica Cistern, Sultanahmet Square is a must-visit destination for anyone interested in Istanbul's rich history and culture.

The history of Sultanahmet Square dates back to the Byzantine era, when it served as the center of the city's political and social life. Originally built as a chariot racing track in the 3rd century, the Hippodrome was later enlarged and adorned with impressive monuments and buildings, such as the

Obelisk of Theodosius and the Serpentine Column.

Today, Sultanahmet Square is a bustling hub of activity, filled with locals and tourists alike. Here are some of the key attractions and experiences you can expect to find in and around the Square:

- The Hagia Sophia: Originally built as a Christian cathedral in the 6th century, the Hagia Sophia is one of Istanbul's most famous landmarks. Today, it serves as a museum, showcasing both Christian and Islamic artwork and architecture.

- The Blue Mosque: With its distinctive six minarets and blue tiles, the Blue Mosque is one of Istanbul's most recognizable landmarks. It's open to visitors outside of prayer times, and visitors are required to remove their shoes and dress modestly.

- The Basilica Cistern: Located just a short walk from Sultanahmet Square, the Basilica Cistern is a massive underground water reservoir that dates back to the Byzantine era. Visitors can explore the dimly lit chambers and marvel at the ornate columns and carvings.

- The Grand Bazaar: Just a short walk from Sultanahmet Square, the Grand Bazaar is one of the largest and oldest covered markets in the world. Here you can find everything from spices and sweets to jewelry and textiles.

- Traditional Turkish cuisine: Sultanahmet Square is home to many restaurants and cafes serving traditional

Turkish cuisine, such as kebabs, meze, and baklava. Don't miss the opportunity to try some of Istanbul's famous street food, such as simit (a sesame-covered bread) or döner (shaved meat served in a pita).

- Street performers and vendors: Sultanahmet Square is a popular spot for street performers and vendors, selling everything from souvenirs to traditional Turkish music performances. Take some time to explore the Square and soak up the vibrant atmosphere.

- The Topkapi Palace: Once the home of the Ottoman sultans, the Topkapi Palace is a sprawling complex of buildings, gardens, and courtyards that offer a glimpse into the opulent lifestyle of the Ottoman Empire.

Visitors can explore the palace's many rooms and exhibits, including the famous Harem.

- The Istanbul Archaeological Museums: Located just a short walk from Sultanahmet Square, the Istanbul Archaeological Museums are a must-visit destination for history buffs. The museums house an impressive collection of ancient artifacts, including the sarcophagus of Alexander the Great and the famed Treaty of Kadesh.

- The Hippodrome Monuments: In addition to the Obelisk of Theodosius and the Serpentine Column, there are several other historic monuments located in Sultanahmet Square. These include the German Fountain, a gift from the German government to the Ottoman Empire, and the Walled

Obelisk, a towering monument adorned with intricate carvings and reliefs.

- The Sokollu Mehmed Pasha Mosque: Located just a short walk from Sultanahmet Square, the Sokollu Mehmed Pasha Mosque is a lesser-known but no less impressive example of Ottoman-era architecture. Built in the 16th century, the mosque features a distinctive octagonal shape and a stunning courtyard with a central fountain.

- The Turkish and Islamic Arts Museum: Located in the nearby neighborhood of Sultanahmet, the Turkish and Islamic Arts Museum is a treasure trove of art, artifacts, and textiles from the Islamic world. Visitors can explore the museum's many exhibits, including rare manuscripts, calligraphy, and ceramics.

- The Bosphorus Cruise: While not located directly in Sultanahmet Square, a Bosphorus cruise is a popular excursion that offers stunning views of Istanbul's skyline and waterfront. Several tour operators offer cruises departing from nearby docks, and many include stops at sites such as the Maiden's Tower and the Dolmabahce Palace.

As with any tourist destination, it's important to be aware of your surroundings and take necessary precautions to stay safe. Pickpocketing and scams can be common in busy tourist areas, so be sure to keep an eye on your belongings and only use reputable tour operators and vendors. With a little bit of caution and common sense, however, Sultanahmet Square is a magical place to explore and discover the rich history and culture of Istanbul.

The Blue Mosque: A Guide to Istanbul's Most Iconic Mosque

The Blue Mosque, also known as the Sultan Ahmed Mosque, is one of Istanbul's most iconic landmarks. Located in the historic Sultanahmet district, the mosque is a testament to the rich history and culture of Istanbul. Here's a guide to everything you need to know about visiting the Blue Mosque:

History and Architecture
The Blue Mosque was built in the early 17th century during the reign of Sultan Ahmed I. The mosque was designed by the famous Ottoman architect, Sedefkâr Mehmed Ağa, and is widely regarded as one of the finest examples of Ottoman-era architecture. The mosque gets its nickname, "The Blue

Mosque," from the thousands of blue tiles that adorn its interior walls.

The mosque is a perfect example of Islamic architecture, with its large central dome, two minarets, and numerous smaller domes. The mosque's interior is also a masterpiece of design, with intricately detailed calligraphy and arabesque designs adorning the walls and ceiling.

Visiting the Blue Mosque
The Blue Mosque is open to visitors every day except during prayer times, which can vary depending on the season. Visitors are welcome to enter the mosque and explore its many halls and courtyards. However, there are some rules that visitors should keep in mind:

- Dress Code: As with most mosques, visitors are required to dress modestly.

This means covering your shoulders, legs, and head (for women). Scarves are available at the mosque entrance for those who need them.

- Shoes: Visitors must remove their shoes before entering the mosque. Shoe storage is available at the entrance.

- Silence: The mosque is an active place of worship, so visitors are asked to speak softly and avoid making loud noises.

Exploring the Mosque

Once inside the Blue Mosque, visitors can explore the main prayer hall, which is open to the public. The main prayer hall is adorned with stunning blue tiles, intricate calligraphy, and ornate chandeliers. Visitors can also explore the numerous side rooms and courtyards, which offer additional examples of Islamic design and art.

It's important to remember that the Blue Mosque is an active place of worship, so visitors are asked to be respectful of those who come to pray. Visitors are also encouraged to take their time and appreciate the mosque's beauty and history.

Nearby Attractions
The Blue Mosque is located in the heart of the Sultanahmet district, which is home to several other notable attractions. Just a short walk from the mosque, visitors can explore the Hagia Sophia, the Topkapi Palace, and the Hippodrome.

Conclusion
The Blue Mosque is a must-visit destination for anyone traveling to Istanbul. With its stunning architecture, rich history, and

intricate design, the mosque offers a unique glimpse into the cultural and religious heritage of Istanbul. Whether you're a history buff, an art lover, or simply looking to soak up the atmosphere of one of Istanbul's most iconic landmarks, the Blue Mosque is a must-see attraction.

Hagia Sophia: A History and Tour of the Ancient Church and Mosque

The Hagia Sophia, also known as the Ayasofya, is one of Istanbul's most iconic landmarks. This ancient church-turned-mosque is a testament to the city's rich history and culture. Here's a guide to the history and tour of the Hagia Sophia:

History
The Hagia Sophia was built in the 6th century by the Byzantine emperor Justinian I. At the time, it was the largest cathedral in the world and served as the center of Eastern Orthodox Christianity for centuries. The building's stunning architecture and intricate mosaics quickly made it one of the world's most important religious buildings.

In 1453, the Ottoman Empire conquered Constantinople (modern-day Istanbul) and the Hagia Sophia was converted into a mosque. Islamic elements were added to the building, including minarets and calligraphy, but the building's original architecture and artwork were largely preserved.

In 1935, the Hagia Sophia was turned into a museum and remained so for over 80 years. However, in 2020, the Turkish government announced that it would be converted back into a mosque, a decision that was met with controversy.

Touring the Hagia Sophia
Visitors to the Hagia Sophia can explore its many halls, courtyards, and galleries. Here are some of the highlights of a tour:

- The Great Hall: The main hall of the Hagia Sophia is breathtaking, with its massive dome and intricate artwork. Visitors can take in the beauty of the building's architecture and gaze up at the dome, which has been compared to the heavens.

- Mosaics: The Hagia Sophia is home to numerous mosaics, many of which date back to the 6th century. These intricate works of art depict biblical scenes, saints, and emperors. While some of the mosaics were covered during the building's time as a mosque, many have been restored and are visible to visitors today.

- Minarets: When the Hagia Sophia was converted into a mosque, several minarets were added to the building. Visitors can climb to the top of these towers for stunning views of the city and the surrounding area.

- Imperial Gate: The Imperial Gate is one of the most ornate entrances to the Hagia Sophia. Visitors can admire its intricate carvings and beautiful marble.

- The Tombs: The Hagia Sophia is home to several tombs, including the tombs of several sultans and their families. Visitors can pay their respects and learn about the lives and legacies of these important figures in Turkish history.

- The Dome: The Hagia Sophia's massive dome is one of the most impressive features of the building. Visitors can admire the intricate patterns and artwork that adorn the interior of the dome, and even take a peek at the galleries located inside.

- The Library: The Hagia Sophia's library is a beautiful and peaceful space that is often overlooked by visitors. The library is home to many ancient manuscripts and books, and visitors can relax and soak in the serene atmosphere.

- Sound and Light Show: The Hagia Sophia offers a unique sound and light show that is not to be missed. The show uses projections and sound effects to bring the building's history to life, and is a great way to learn more about Hagia Sophia's rich heritage.

Tips for Visitors

- Dress Code: Visitors should dress modestly when visiting the Hagia Sophia. This means covering your shoulders and legs.

- Shoes: Visitors must remove their shoes before entering the mosque. Shoe storage is available at the entrance.

- Crowds: The Hagia Sophia can be very crowded, particularly during peak tourist season. Visitors should plan to arrive early to avoid long lines.

- Audio Guide: An audio guide is available for visitors who want to learn more about the history and significance of the Hagia Sophia.

Conclusion

The Hagia Sophia is a must-visit destination for anyone traveling to Istanbul. With its rich history, stunning architecture, and intricate artwork, the building offers a unique glimpse into the cultural and religious heritage of Istanbul. Whether you're a history buff, an art lover, or simply looking to soak up the atmosphere of one of Istanbul's most iconic landmarks, the Hagia Sophia is a must-see attraction.

Topkapi Palace: Discovering the Grandeur of Ottoman Architecture and Design

Topkapi Palace, located in the heart of Istanbul, is one of the most impressive and grand structures in the city. It was the residence of the Ottoman sultans for almost 400 years, and is now one of the most popular tourist destinations in Istanbul. Visitors can spend hours exploring the palace's many rooms, gardens, and courtyards, and marveling at the intricate architecture and design.

The palace is divided into several sections, each with its own unique character and history. One of the most impressive parts of the palace is the Imperial Harem, which was home to the sultan's wives, concubines, and children. Visitors can explore the many rooms and courtyards of the Harem, and learn about the daily life of the palace's female residents.

Another highlight of Topkapi Palace is the Treasury, which houses a vast collection of precious jewels, gold, and other treasures. Visitors can admire the many ornate objects on display, including the famous Topkapi Dagger, which is encrusted with emeralds, rubies, and diamonds.

The palace's many gardens and courtyards are also worth exploring. The Imperial Council Hall, for example, is a large open-air space where the sultan would meet with his advisors and ministers. Visitors can take in the stunning views of the Bosphorus and the city from the terrace, and imagine what it must have been like to hold court in such a grand setting.

Other highlights of the palace include the Palace Kitchens, where the sultan's elaborate meals were prepared, and the Sultan's Apartments, which offer a glimpse into the private living quarters of the sultan and his family.

Overall, Topkapi Palace is a must-visit destination for anyone interested in Ottoman history and architecture. The palace's grandeur and opulence are a testament to the power and wealth of the Ottoman Empire, and visitors can spend hours exploring its many treasures and hidden corners. Whether you are a history buff, an architecture enthusiast, or simply looking for a beautiful and inspiring place to visit, Topkapi Palace is sure to delight and inspire.

Another popular attraction within Topkapi Palace is the Sacred Relics collection. This collection contains a number of significant religious artifacts, including the Prophet Muhammad's cloak and sword, and the staff of Moses. The collection is located in the palace's Chamber of the Sacred Relics, and is considered one of the most important collections of Islamic artifacts in the world.

Visitors to Topkapi Palace can also enjoy stunning views of the Bosphorus and the city of Istanbul from the palace's many terraces and courtyards. The palace's gardens are also a popular spot for visitors to relax and enjoy the beautiful surroundings.

To make the most of your visit to Topkapi Palace, it's a good idea to plan ahead and give yourself plenty of time to explore. Guided tours are available, and can be a great way to learn more about the palace's history and significance. Be sure to wear comfortable shoes and clothing, as the palace grounds can be quite large and involve a fair amount of walking.

Overall, Topkapi Palace is a must-visit destination for anyone traveling to Istanbul. Its grandeur, beauty, and historical significance make it one of the city's most iconic landmarks, and a place that visitors will remember long after their trip has ended.

The Grand Bazaar: Navigating Istanbul's Famous Marketplace

The Grand Bazaar in Istanbul is one of the largest and oldest covered markets in the world, and a must-visit destination for anyone traveling to the city. With more than 4,000 shops spread out over 60 streets and alleys, the bazaar can be overwhelming for first-time visitors. But with a little planning and patience, navigating this sprawling marketplace can be a fun and rewarding experience.

The bazaar's history dates back to the 15th century, and it has been an important commercial center in Istanbul ever since. The market is divided into several sections, each with its own unique character and offerings. Visitors can find everything from jewelry and textiles to ceramics and spices, and bargaining is a common practice.

One of the most important things to keep in mind when visiting the Grand Bazaar is to arrive early in the day, when the market is less crowded and the shopkeepers are more eager to make a sale. It's also a good idea to come with a plan in mind, as the bazaar can be overwhelming and it's easy to get lost. It's helpful to have a map of the market, or to hire a guide to help you navigate the labyrinth of shops and alleys.

When shopping in the Grand Bazaar, it's important to remember that haggling is a common practice. Prices are not fixed, and shopkeepers will often offer a higher price to start with. Negotiating is part of the shopping experience, so don't be afraid to ask for a lower price, but be respectful and polite in your interactions.

In addition to shopping, the Grand Bazaar is also a great place to soak up the atmosphere and culture of Istanbul. The market is full of colorful characters, from the shopkeepers to the local shoppers, and there are plenty of opportunities to sample traditional Turkish cuisine and sweets.

The Grand Bazaar is open from Monday to Saturday, from 9am to 7pm, but it is closed on Sundays and during some public holidays. If you're planning to visit on a weekend or holiday, it's a good idea to arrive early to avoid the crowds. The market can get very busy, especially during peak tourist season, so it's important to be mindful of your surroundings and keep your belongings close.

When shopping at the Grand Bazaar, it's important to keep in mind that quality and authenticity can vary greatly. Some shops may sell knock-off products, while others may sell genuine items at a higher price. It's important to do your research beforehand and be cautious when purchasing high-value items such as gold or jewelry. If you're unsure about a shop or item, don't hesitate to ask for a certificate of authenticity or get a second opinion.

The Grand Bazaar is also a great place to explore Istanbul's cultural heritage. Many of the shops offer traditional Turkish products, such as carpets, ceramics, and textiles, that are handmade using traditional methods. You can also find local products like spices and sweets that are unique to Turkey. Be sure to take some time to explore the smaller alleys and side streets, where you can find hidden gems and local artisans.

If you need a break from shopping, there are plenty of cafes and restaurants in and around the Grand Bazaar where you can relax and refuel. Try traditional Turkish dishes like kebabs, pide (Turkish pizza), or baklava, a sweet pastry made with phyllo dough, nuts, and syrup.

Overall, the Grand Bazaar is a must-see destination for anyone visiting Istanbul. Its unique atmosphere, cultural heritage, and diverse shopping experiences make it a highlight of any trip to the city. Whether you're looking to shop for souvenirs, sample local cuisine, or simply soak up the sights and sounds of this bustling market, the Grand Bazaar is sure to leave a lasting impression.

Best Bars in Istanbul

Istanbul's nightlife scene is as varied as the city itself, with a range of options to suit all tastes and budgets. Here, we take a look at some of the best bars in Istanbul, each offering its own unique atmosphere, drinks, and menu items.

- 360 Istanbul: Located on the top floor of a building in Beyoglu, 360 Istanbul offers panoramic views of the city, making it a popular spot for both tourists and locals. The atmosphere is chic and modern, with live music on weekends. The cocktail menu is extensive, with unique offerings like the "Istanbul 360" and "Bosphorus Sunset" cocktails. Prices are on the high end, with cocktails averaging around 50-60 TL (around $6-7 USD).

- Arsen Lupen: This cozy bar in the Galata neighborhood has a speakeasy vibe, with a dimly lit interior and eclectic decor. The drink menu is creative and often changes with the season, with options like the "Lavender Martini" and "Smokey Old Fashioned." The food menu is also worth trying, with dishes like the "Truffle Mac and Cheese" and "Duck Ragu." Prices are mid-range, with cocktails averaging around 35-40 TL (around $4-5 USD).

- Peyote: A popular bar in the trendy Karakoy neighborhood, Peyote is known for its industrial-chic decor and creative cocktails. The menu is extensive, with options like the "Basil Smash" and "Peyote Margarita." The bar also serves small plates and sandwiches, like the "Smoked Chicken Sandwich" and "Truffle Fries." Prices are on the higher side, with cocktails averaging around 45-50 TL (around $5-6 USD).

- Taps Bebek: Taps Bebek is a spacious and lively bar located in the upscale Bebek neighborhood, with an outdoor terrace overlooking the Bosphorus. The bar offers a variety of local and imported beers, as well as cocktails and wine. The food menu features pub favorites like burgers and nachos, as well as Turkish specialties like "Izmir Kofte" and "Beykoz Kebab." Prices are mid-range, with beers averaging around 20-25 TL (around $2-3 USD) and cocktails around 35-40 TL (around $4-5 USD).

- Kiki Ortakoy: This bar in the Ortakoy neighborhood is known for its lively atmosphere and variety of cocktails.

The menu features classic options like the "Mojito" and "Cosmopolitan," as well as unique creations like the "Pineapple and Thyme Martini." The food menu is limited but includes small bites like "Chili Cheese Bites" and "Garlic Bread." Prices are mid-range, with cocktails averaging around 30-35 TL (around $3-4 USD).

When visiting these bars, keep in mind a few general etiquette guidelines for enjoying Istanbul's nightlife. Dress codes vary by location, with some bars requiring more formal attire while others are more casual. It's also important to be respectful of local customs and avoid excessive public displays of affection. Finally, be aware of your surroundings and take precautions to stay safe, especially when traveling alone or late at night. Overall, Istanbul's nightlife offers a range of exciting and unique options for visitors to enjoy.

Best Clubs in Istanbul

Istanbul is a city that truly comes alive after dark, and the club scene is no exception. From techno and house to Turkish pop and traditional folk music, there's a club for every taste in Istanbul. Here's a guide to some of the best clubs in the city:

- Zorlu Center PSM - This multi-level venue is one of the hottest spots in Istanbul, with a range of genres and events catering to a diverse crowd. From electronic dance music to live performances by Turkish artists, Zorlu Center PSM has it all. The dress code is casual, and the average cost of entry ranges from 50 to 100 TL ($6 to $12 USD).

- Sortie - Located on the Bosphorus in the trendy Ortakoy neighborhood,

Sortie is known for its beautiful outdoor terrace and Mediterranean-inspired decor. The club offers a mix of house and Turkish pop music, and the dress code is upscale casual. Expect to pay around 50 to 100 TL ($6 to $12 USD) for entry and 25 TL ($3 USD) for a beer.

- Babylon - This iconic Istanbul venue has been around since the 1990s and remains a beloved spot for music lovers. With two locations in Beyoglu, Babylon features everything from jazz and world music to electronic and rock. The atmosphere is casual and laid-back, with a diverse crowd of locals and tourists. Entry fees range from 30 to 100 TL ($4 to $12 USD), depending on the night and event.

- Klein - If you're looking for a more intimate club experience, Klein is the place to be. Located in the historic Galata neighborhood, this underground venue features local DJs spinning techno and house music. The atmosphere is dark and edgy, and the dress code is casual. Expect to pay around 50 to 100 TL ($6 to $12 USD) for entry and 25 TL ($3 USD) for a beer.

- Anjelique - This club is located on the Bosphorus in the Ortakoy neighborhood and offers stunning views of the water and the city skyline. Anjelique is known for its upscale atmosphere and Turkish pop music, as well as occasional international DJs. The dress code is upscale, and entry fees range from 50 to 100 TL ($6 to $12 USD).

- Kiki - This small club in the trendy Cihangir neighborhood is a favorite among locals for its laid-back atmosphere and alternative music scene. Expect to hear everything from indie rock to electronic and hip hop. The dress code is casual, and the average cost of entry is around 30 to 50 TL ($4 to $6 USD).

Overall, the cost of drinks and entry fees in Istanbul's clubs is relatively affordable compared to other major cities. A beer can range from 25 to 35 TL ($3 to $4 USD), while cocktails and shots are around 50 to 75 TL ($6 to $9 USD). Many clubs offer a cover charge that includes a drink or two, and some even offer free entry for women on certain nights. It's also worth noting that most clubs in Istanbul don't get going until after midnight and stay open until the early hours of the morning.

Safety and Etiquette in Istanbul's Nightlife

Istanbul's nightlife scene is a vibrant and exciting experience for both locals and visitors. However, it is important to stay safe and be mindful of the local culture and customs. Here are some essential safety and etiquette tips to keep in mind when enjoying Istanbul's nightlife.

Safety Tips:

- Stick to well-lit and busy areas - Avoid poorly lit and isolated areas, especially at night. Stick to main streets and popular neighborhoods.

- Beware of pickpockets - Keep an eye on your belongings and avoid carrying large amounts of cash or valuable items. Keep your wallet in a secure pocket or a bag that can be closed and carried close to your body.

- Watch your drink - Be careful of accepting drinks from strangers or leaving your drink unattended. This is a common tactic used by thieves and scammers.

- Use trusted transportation - Only use licensed taxis or reputable ride-sharing services like Uber or Bolt.

- Plan your night out in advance - Before heading out, make sure to plan your transportation, identify the locations you want to visit, and share your plans with a trusted friend or family member.

Etiquette Tips:
- Dress appropriately - While Istanbul is a modern city, it is still respectful to

dress modestly, especially when visiting mosques and religious sites. In clubs and bars, the dress code is typically casual or smart casual.

- Respect local customs - Istanbul is a Muslim city, so it's important to respect local customs and traditions, including dress codes and public behavior.

- Learn basic Turkish phrases - Learning some basic Turkish phrases can go a long way in showing respect to the local culture and making new friends.

- Don't be too loud or disruptive - It's important to have fun, but try not to disturb others while doing so. Keep your voice down and avoid rowdy behavior in public areas.

- Be mindful of personal space - In crowded bars and clubs, it's important to be aware of your personal space and respect others around you.

By following these safety and etiquette tips, you can enjoy Istanbul's nightlife while being respectful and staying safe. Remember to always be aware of your surroundings and trust your instincts.

Turkish Breakfast and Brunch

Turkish Breakfast and Brunch: A Guide to the Best Morning Eats in Istanbul

In Turkish culture, breakfast is the most important meal of the day. It is a time to relax, socialize, and enjoy delicious food with family and friends. Turkish breakfast, or "kahvalti," is a feast of sweet and savory dishes that are typically shared around a large table.

Traditional Turkish Breakfast

A typical Turkish breakfast consists of a variety of small plates, including olives, cheese, cucumbers, tomatoes, honey, jams, and fresh bread. Menemen, a type of scrambled eggs with tomatoes, onions, and peppers, is also a popular breakfast dish in Turkey. Another staple of Turkish breakfast is "sucuk," a spicy sausage made from beef or lamb.

One of the best places to experience a traditional Turkish breakfast is at Van Kahvalti Evi, located in the Cihangir neighborhood of Istanbul. This restaurant serves an extensive breakfast spread, including homemade jams, fresh cheese, and warm flatbreads. The cozy atmosphere and friendly staff make it a perfect spot to start your day.

For a more upscale Turkish breakfast experience, visit the Four Seasons Hotel Istanbul at the Bosphorus. The hotel offers a breakfast buffet that includes fresh juices, cheeses, cold cuts, and Turkish pastries. Guests can enjoy their meal on a terrace overlooking the Bosphorus, with the sound of the waves and seagulls in the background.

Brunch in Istanbul

If you're looking for a more modern take on breakfast, Istanbul has many options for brunch. Mangerie Bebek, located in the Bebek neighborhood, offers a Mediterranean-inspired brunch menu that includes everything from poached eggs to avocado toast. The restaurant has a beautiful terrace with a view of the Bosphorus, making it a popular spot for locals and tourists alike.

Another popular brunch spot in Istanbul is Nopa, located in the trendy Karakoy neighborhood. The menu features dishes such as shakshuka, grilled halloumi, and Turkish-style pancakes with honey and kaymak, a type of clotted cream. The industrial-chic decor and lively atmosphere make Nopa a great place to spend a lazy Sunday morning.

Safety and Etiquette

As with any nightlife experience, it's important to be aware of your surroundings and take precautions to stay safe. Avoid walking alone late at night and never leave your drink unattended. Be cautious of scams, such as people offering to take you to a club or bar and then charging you an exorbitant fee.

It's also important to respect local customs and etiquette when enjoying Istanbul's nightlife. Dress modestly and avoid wearing revealing clothing or overly flashy jewelry. When interacting with locals and fellow tourists, be polite and respectful. Learning a few basic Turkish phrases, such as "merhaba" (hello) and "teşekkür ederim" (thank you), can go a long way in showing respect for the culture.

In conclusion, Turkish breakfast and brunch are not to be missed when visiting Istanbul. Whether you're looking for a traditional breakfast spread or a more modern brunch experience, Istanbul has something for everyone. Just remember to stay safe and respect local customs and etiquette when enjoying the city's vibrant nightlife.

Street Food

Istanbul is a city that is famous for its culinary delights, and one of the best ways to experience its food culture is through its vibrant street food scene. The streets of Istanbul are lined with vendors selling all kinds of delicious treats that are both affordable and flavorful. In this guide, we'll take a look at some of the most popular street food options in Istanbul, where to find the best street food vendors in the city, tips for eating street food safely, and an overview of classic street food dishes.

Popular Street Food Options in Istanbul
Istanbul's street food scene is diverse, and there are many different options to choose from. Some of the most popular street food options include:

- Simit: A circular bread with a crunchy exterior and a soft interior, covered in sesame seeds.

- Doner Kebab: Thinly sliced meat cooked on a vertical rotisserie, served in a pita or wrap with vegetables and sauce.

- Balik Ekmek: Grilled fish served on bread with lettuce, onions, and tomatoes.

- Kumpir: A baked potato that is mashed and mixed with butter and cheese, then topped with various toppings such as olives, corn, and pickles.

- Lahmacun: A thin flatbread topped with minced meat, vegetables, and spices.

Where to Find the Best Street Food Vendors in Istanbul

One of the best things about Istanbul's street food scene is that vendors can be found all over the city. Some of the most popular areas for street food include:

- Taksim Square: The heart of Istanbul's entertainment and nightlife district, where you can find all kinds of food vendors.

- Karakoy: A historic neighborhood that has become a trendy spot for street food, including fish sandwiches.

- Eminonu: A busy port area that is famous for its fish sandwiches and other seafood dishes.

- Kadikoy: A neighborhood on the Asian side of the city that is known for its street food and markets.

Guidelines for Safe Street Food Consumption
While street food is a great way to experience Istanbul's food culture, it's important to take some precautions to avoid getting sick. For safe street food consumption, consider the following advice:

- Look for busy vendors: Busy vendors are likely to have high turnover, which means the food is fresh and safe to eat.

- Check for hygiene: Look for vendors who handle food with clean hands and use gloves or utensils.

- Avoid uncooked food: Raw or undercooked food can be a breeding ground for bacteria, so make sure your food is fully cooked.

- Bring hand sanitizer: Hand sanitizer can help you avoid getting sick from any bacteria on your hands after handling money or touching other surfaces.

Classic Street Food Dishes

Here are some classic street food dishes you shouldn't miss out on:

- Simit: A simple yet satisfying snack that's perfect for breakfast or a midday snack.

- Doner Kebab: One of the most popular dishes in Istanbul, doner kebab is a must-try for any visitor.

- Balik Ekmek: A fresh and delicious sandwich that's perfect for a lunch by the water.

- Kumpir: A hearty and filling dish that's perfect for a quick and satisfying meal.

- Lahmacun: A great option for a light and flavorful meal or snack.

In conclusion, Istanbul's street food scene is a must-try for anyone visiting the city. With so many options to choose from, you're sure to find something that satisfies your taste buds. Just be sure to follow some basic safety guidelines and take some precautions to avoid getting sick, so you can fully enjoy all the delicious flavors the city has to offer.

Seafood

Istanbul is a city that has long been influenced by the sea, making its seafood offerings a must-try for any foodie. From classic meze to fresh fish, Istanbul's seafood scene has something to offer for everyone.

Seafood is an essential part of Istanbul's culinary tradition, and for centuries the city has relied on the sea for its livelihood. With the Bosphorus strait cutting through the city and the Sea of Marmara to the south, Istanbul has access to an abundance of fresh fish and other seafood. This means that seafood is not only a delicious and healthy food option, but it's also readily available and affordable.

Istanbul's seafood restaurants offer a wide range of options, from classic fish dishes to modern seafood fusion cuisine. Classic dishes include grilled fish, served simply with a side of vegetables or salad, as well as meze platters with a variety of small dishes like marinated anchovies, stuffed mussels, and octopus salad.

For those looking for a more modern take on seafood, Istanbul has several trendy seafood restaurants that offer fusion cuisine, like sushi rolls filled with local fish or dishes that blend Mediterranean and Turkish flavors.

When looking for the best seafood restaurants in Istanbul, it's important to seek out those that serve fresh, sustainably caught fish. Some popular options include Balikci Sabahattin, a classic restaurant near the Spice Bazaar, or the trendy and sustainable Mikla, located on the rooftop of the Marmara Pera hotel. Both restaurants have great reputations and offer delicious and high-quality seafood dishes.

If you want to try seafood street food, Istanbul has a few popular dishes worth trying, such as balik ekmek, which is a sandwich of grilled fish and salad, and midye dolma, which is a stuffed mussel with rice and spices. These street foods can be found at vendors along the Bosphorus or at local food markets like Kadikoy or Besiktas.

When it comes to choosing the freshest seafood options, look for restaurants that offer daily specials based on the catch of the day, and avoid places that offer seafood dishes that seem too cheap or too good to be true. It's also important to take food safety precautions when eating seafood in Istanbul, such as avoiding raw or undercooked dishes and sticking to bottled water instead of tap water.

In conclusion, Istanbul's seafood scene is a must-try for any foodie. From classic meze to trendy fusion dishes, the city offers a wide range of options for seafood lovers. With so many delicious and high-quality restaurants to choose from, as well as unique street food options, it's easy to see why seafood is such an important and beloved part of Istanbul's culinary tradition.

Cost of living in Istanbul

Istanbul is a vibrant and diverse city that attracts both tourists and expats from all over the world. While the cost of living in Istanbul is generally lower than other major European cities, it is still important to consider your budget when planning your trip or relocation. Here is an overview of the cost of living in Istanbul:

Accommodation:
The cost of accommodation in Istanbul can vary greatly depending on the neighborhood and type of accommodation. A basic one-bedroom apartment in the city center can cost between 3,000-5,000 TRY per month, while a three-bedroom apartment can cost up to 10,000 TRY. Prices outside of the city center are generally lower.

Food and Drinks:

Istanbul offers a wide range of food options at varying prices. Local street food and casual restaurants can be very affordable, with prices starting from 20 TRY per meal. Fine dining and international cuisine can be more expensive, with prices averaging around 150-200 TRY per meal. The cost of alcoholic drinks is also reasonable, with a beer costing between 15-30 TRY and a cocktail averaging around 50-60 TRY.

Transportation:
Istanbul has a well-developed public transportation system that includes buses, trams, metro, and ferries. A single ride on public transportation costs 5 TRY, and a monthly pass can be purchased for around 300 TRY. Taxis are also available, with prices starting from 4.50 TRY per km.

Entertainment:

Istanbul offers a wide range of entertainment options, including museums, art galleries, theaters, and sports events. Prices for these activities vary, with most museums and galleries charging between 25-50 TRY for admission. Sports events and concerts can be more expensive, with prices ranging from 100-500 TRY.

Overall, the cost of living in Istanbul is relatively affordable when compared to other major European cities. However, it is still important to plan your budget carefully to ensure you can enjoy all the city has to offer without breaking the bank.

Bosphorus Cruise: A Journey Through Istanbul's Waterways and Scenic Views

A Bosphorus Cruise is one of the most popular activities for tourists visiting Istanbul, and for good reason. This breathtaking journey takes you through the waterways of Istanbul, offering stunning views of the city's architecture and natural landscapes.

The Bosphorus Strait is a narrow waterway that separates the European and Asian sides of Istanbul, and it's a hub of activity for both locals and tourists. The cruise typically starts from the Eminonu or Kabatas port on the European side, and passes by some of Istanbul's most iconic landmarks, such as the Dolmabahce Palace, the Bosphorus Bridge, and the Maiden's Tower.

One of the best parts of the Bosphorus Cruise is the opportunity to see the city from a different perspective. You'll get to enjoy panoramic views of Istanbul's skyline, and see how the city's architecture blends Ottoman, Byzantine, and modern influences. Along the way, you'll also see a variety of neighborhoods, from the historic mansions of the Ottoman elite to the trendy cafes and restaurants that line the shores.

The Bosphorus is also rich in natural beauty, with rolling hills, lush forests, and scenic coves along the way. You might see fishermen casting their lines, dolphins swimming alongside the boat, or even sea turtles sunning themselves on the rocks. It's a great opportunity to take in the sights, sounds, and smells of Istanbul's waterways.

The duration and itinerary of Bosphorus Cruises can vary, from short one-hour tours to longer sunset or dinner cruises. Some boats even offer live entertainment, such as traditional Turkish music and dancing. Regardless of the type of cruise you choose, it's important to dress comfortably and bring sunscreen, as it can get quite sunny on the water.

In addition to the traditional Bosphorus Cruise, there are also private yacht and boat tours available for a more intimate experience. These tours offer a more personalized approach, with customizable routes and stops along the way. You can work with the tour company to create a custom itinerary that suits your preferences, whether it's a longer journey up the Bosphorus or a shorter trip around the Golden Horn.

For those interested in history and culture, some boat tours also offer a guided commentary about Istanbul's past and present. You'll learn about the significance of the landmarks you pass by, and gain a deeper understanding of Istanbul's unique place in the world.

If you're interested in taking a sunset or dinner cruise, you'll be treated to a breathtaking view of Istanbul's skyline as the sun sets over the water. This is a romantic and unforgettable experience, perfect for couples looking for a special night out.

No matter which type of Bosphorus Cruise you choose, it's important to keep in mind that the water can be choppy at times, especially in the afternoons when the sea breeze picks up. Be sure to bring a light jacket or scarf to stay warm, and hold on to your belongings tightly. And don't forget to bring your camera to capture the beautiful scenery along the way!

Overall, a Bosphorus Cruise is a memorable and relaxing way to experience Istanbul's beauty and charm. Whether you're looking for a romantic evening with your partner or a fun family activity, a cruise through Istanbul's waterways is sure to be a highlight of your trip.

Dolmabahce Palace: A Tour of Istanbul's European-Style Palace and Gardens

Located on the European side of Istanbul, Dolmabahce Palace is a magnificent example of European-style architecture and design that served as the administrative center of the Ottoman Empire from 1856 to 1922. The palace was built in the mid-19th century during a time when Ottoman leaders sought to modernize their empire and emulate Western Europe.

The palace features a unique blend of Baroque, Rococo, and Neoclassical styles, with elaborate chandeliers, ornate ceiling frescoes, and grand staircases. The palace's 285 rooms are spread across three floors and include opulent reception halls, state rooms, and private living quarters for the sultan and his family.

One of the most impressive features of the palace is the Crystal Staircase, a grand staircase made of Baccarat crystal and brass that leads to the state rooms. Other notable rooms include the Medhal (entrance hall), the Ceremonial Hall, the Throne Room, and the Crystal Gallery, which houses one of the largest Bohemian crystal chandeliers in the world.

The palace's gardens are also a sight to behold, with manicured lawns, colorful flower beds, and a stunning view of the Bosphorus. The palace grounds also feature the Dolmabahce Clock Tower, a gift from the French in the 19th century, and a mosque with an impressive dome and two minarets.

Guided tours are available to visitors, offering a glimpse into the palace's rich history and architecture. The tours typically last around 1-2 hours and cover the most important rooms and features of the palace. Visitors are also free to explore the gardens and grounds at their leisure.

It's important to note that photography is not allowed inside the palace, and visitors must remove their shoes before entering. Additionally, certain areas of the palace may be closed to visitors during official state ceremonies or events.

Dolmabahce Palace was designed by Armenian architects Garabet Balyan and his son Nigogayos Balyan, who were renowned for their contributions to the Ottoman architecture. The construction of the palace took 13 years and was completed in 1856, costing an exorbitant amount of money at the time. The palace was built to replace the old Topkapi Palace, which was deemed outdated and insufficient for the needs of the modernizing Ottoman Empire.

The palace was also the residence of the last Ottoman sultan, Mehmed VI, who was forced to leave the palace in 1922 following the collapse of the Ottoman Empire. The palace was then used as the presidential residence by Mustafa Kemal Ataturk, the founder of modern Turkey, until his death in 1938.

Today, Dolmabahce Palace is one of Istanbul's most popular tourist destinations, attracting visitors from all over the world. The palace is open to the public every day except Mondays and Thursdays, and tickets can be purchased at the entrance. Visitors are advised to arrive early to avoid long queues, especially during peak tourist seasons.

In addition to the palace, there are several other attractions in the area that are worth visiting. The Dolmabahce Mosque, located next to the palace, is a beautiful example of Ottoman architecture and features intricate tilework, a marble fountain, and stunning stained-glass windows. The Besiktas Fish Market is also nearby, offering a wide variety of fresh seafood and local delicacies.

Whether you're a history buff, an architecture enthusiast, or simply looking for a beautiful place to explore, Dolmabahce Palace is a must-visit destination in Istanbul. Its grandeur and beauty make it an unforgettable experience, and its rich history and cultural significance are sure to leave a lasting impression.

Taksim Square: Exploring the Modern Side of Istanbul

Taksim Square is located in the heart of Istanbul's modern district, and it is one of the city's most iconic landmarks. The square is named after the taksim, or water distribution point, which once stood in the area during the Ottoman period.

Taksim Square is a bustling hub of activity, with numerous restaurants, cafes, and shops lining the streets. The area is also home to several hotels and nightlife venues, making it a popular destination for tourists and locals alike.

One of the most recognizable landmarks in Taksim Square is the Monument of the Republic, which was erected in 1928 to commemorate the founding of the Turkish

Republic. The monument features a large statue of Mustafa Kemal Ataturk, the founder of modern Turkey, and it is often used as a gathering point for political rallies and demonstrations.

Another notable feature of Taksim Square is the Istiklal Avenue, a pedestrian street lined with shops, cafes, and historic buildings. The avenue is the busiest shopping street in Istanbul and attracts millions of visitors each year.

Taksim Square is also home to several cultural and artistic institutions, including the Ataturk Cultural Center, which hosts concerts, theater performances, and art exhibitions. The Istanbul Modern Art Museum is also located nearby, featuring a collection of contemporary art from Turkey and around the world.

Visitors to Taksim Square can also take a ride on the historic Taksim tram, which runs along Istiklal Avenue and provides a scenic tour of the area. The tram is a popular attraction for both tourists and locals and is often used as a backdrop for photographs and selfies.

In addition to its bustling street life and cultural offerings, Taksim Square is also an important transportation hub in Istanbul. The square is served by several bus lines and the Taksim metro station, which provides easy access to other parts of the city.

At night, Taksim Square comes alive with a vibrant nightlife scene, with numerous bars, clubs, and music venues catering to a diverse range of tastes. The area is especially popular with young people, who flock to the area to socialize and enjoy the lively atmosphere.

One of the most popular events in Taksim Square is the annual New Year's Eve celebration, which draws thousands of people to the area to ring in the new year with live music, fireworks, and a festive atmosphere.

Despite its modernity, Taksim Square is also home to several historic landmarks and buildings, including the Ataturk Cultural Center, which was built in the 1960s and is considered a prime example of modernist architecture in Turkey. The square is also home to several historic churches and synagogues, reflecting the city's diverse religious heritage.

Whether you're interested in shopping, dining, culture, or nightlife, Taksim Square is a must-visit destination in Istanbul, offering a unique blend of modernity and history in the heart of the city.

Istiklal Avenue: A Stroll Through Istanbul's Bustling Shopping and Entertainment District

Istiklal Avenue is a lively pedestrian street in the heart of Istanbul, known for its vibrant mix of shopping, entertainment, and cultural attractions. It's a must-see destination for visitors to the city, offering a glimpse into the modern side of Istanbul.

The street stretches for about three kilometers, from Taksim Square in the north to the Galata Tower in the south, and is lined with a variety of shops, restaurants, cafes, and galleries. From international fashion brands to local boutiques, Istiklal Avenue has something for everyone.

The avenue is also home to a number of historic landmarks, including the Galatasaray High School, which dates back to the 19th century, and the St. Anthony of Padua Church, a beautiful Catholic church built in the early 20th century.

In addition to its shopping and cultural offerings, Istiklal Avenue is also a popular nightlife destination. The street comes alive at night, with a variety of bars and clubs offering music, drinks, and entertainment for all tastes.

To experience Istiklal Avenue to the fullest, it's best to visit on foot, taking in the sights, sounds, and smells of this bustling district. And if you're looking for a break from the hustle and bustle, there are several parks and green spaces nearby where you can relax and unwind.

One of the most unique aspects of Istiklal Avenue is its historic red tram, which runs the length of the street and provides a fun and nostalgic way to explore the area. The tram is a popular photo opportunity for visitors and locals alike, and offers a convenient way to get around Istiklal Avenue.

Another attraction of Istiklal Avenue is the impressive Istanbul Modern Art Museum, which showcases works by Turkish and international contemporary artists. The museum is housed in a converted warehouse, and offers a unique and modern contrast to the historic surroundings of the avenue.

For foodies, Istiklal Avenue is a great place to sample traditional Turkish cuisine, as well as international cuisine from all over the world. From street food vendors selling simit (a type of Turkish bagel) and roasted chestnuts, to upscale restaurants serving meze (a variety of small dishes), grilled meats, and other specialties, there's something to suit every taste and budget.

Istiklal Avenue is also known for its street performers, who can be found entertaining crowds throughout the day and into the night. From musicians and dancers to acrobats and magicians, the avenue offers a lively and entertaining atmosphere that's hard to beat.

Overall, Istiklal Avenue is a must-visit destination for anyone traveling to Istanbul, offering a unique mix of history, culture, entertainment, and shopping. Whether you're interested in exploring the area's rich heritage, sampling local cuisine, or simply soaking up the vibrant atmosphere, there's something for everyone on Istiklal Avenue.

Galata Tower: A Panoramic View of Istanbul's Skyline and History

Galata Tower is a must-see attraction for visitors to Istanbul, offering breathtaking panoramic views of the city's skyline and an opportunity to step back in time to experience the tower's fascinating history.

Located in the historic district of Beyoğlu, Galata Tower was built in 1348 as part of the Genoese citadel that once stood in the area. The tower was originally used as a lookout post and to house prisoners, and has undergone many renovations and additions throughout its long history.

Today, visitors can climb to the top of the tower to take in stunning views of Istanbul's Old City, the Bosphorus Strait, and the modern skyline of the city. On a clear day, you can see as far as the Princes' Islands, the Golden Horn, and the Marmara Sea. There is also a restaurant and cafe at the top of the tower, where visitors can enjoy a meal or a drink while taking in the stunning views.

In addition to its impressive views, Galata Tower also boasts a rich history that can be explored in the tower's museum. Visitors can learn about the tower's various uses throughout history, from a watchtower and prison to a fire observation post and radio station. The museum also includes displays on the history of Istanbul and the surrounding area, providing context for the tower's significance in the city's history.

Another interesting feature of Galata Tower is the traditional Turkish dance and music performances that are held there in the evenings. Visitors can enjoy dinner and a show while taking in the stunning views from the tower's observation deck.

In addition to its history and stunning views, Galata Tower also serves as a landmark for Istanbul's vibrant and dynamic culture. The tower is located in one of Istanbul's liveliest neighborhoods, and visitors can explore the surrounding area to get a taste of the city's modern culture and entertainment.

The streets around Galata Tower are filled with trendy cafes, restaurants, and shops, as well as art galleries and theaters. The neighborhood is known for its vibrant nightlife, with many bars and clubs staying open late into the night. Visitors can take a stroll down the lively Istiklal Avenue or explore the hip streets of Karaköy to get a taste of the area's unique culture and entertainment scene.

More importantly, Galata Tower has served as a source of inspiration for many artists and writers throughout history. It has been depicted in countless paintings, photographs, and literature, and has become an iconic symbol of Istanbul's rich history and cultural significance.

For those interested in learning more about the tower's history and significance, there are also guided tours available that provide in-depth information and context about the tower's past and present. These tours can help visitors gain a deeper understanding of Istanbul's cultural and historical significance and make the most of their visit to this iconic landmark.

Overall, a visit to Galata Tower is an essential part of any trip to Istanbul. Whether you're interested in history, culture, or stunning views of the city, the tower offers a unique and unforgettable experience that's sure to leave a lasting impression.

Spice Bazaar: Discovering Istanbul's Exotic Flavors and Aromas

The Spice Bazaar, also known as the Egyptian Bazaar, is one of Istanbul's most iconic and colorful markets, offering a sensory explosion of exotic flavors and aromas. Located in the heart of the city, the bazaar has been a center of trade and commerce for centuries, and remains a bustling hub of activity today.

As soon as you enter the Spice Bazaar, you are met with an overwhelming array of colors and scents, from the earthy smell of cumin to the sweet aroma of Turkish delight. The market is filled with vendors selling a wide variety of spices, herbs, teas, and other culinary delights, as well as souvenirs and gifts.

The Spice Bazaar is an excellent place to sample and purchase authentic Turkish food and ingredients, such as Turkish saffron, sumac, and Aleppo pepper. You can also find a variety of dried fruits and nuts, Turkish coffee, and traditional sweets like baklava and lokum (Turkish delight).

In addition to the food and spices, the Spice Bazaar is also a great place to soak up the local culture and traditions. The vendors are friendly and welcoming, and many are happy to share their knowledge and expertise with visitors. You can learn about the history and uses of different spices, as well as traditional cooking methods and recipes.

The Spice Bazaar is a popular destination for tourists, but it's also a favorite spot among locals, who come here to purchase their daily spices and ingredients. The best time to visit the market is in the morning, when it's at its busiest and most vibrant.

The Spice Bazaar,is a vibrant and bustling marketplace that has been a fixture in Istanbul since the 17th century. It is located in the Eminönü district, near the Galata Bridge and the New Mosque, making it a popular destination for tourists and locals alike.

As soon as you enter the bazaar, you'll be greeted by the heady aroma of spices, herbs, and teas. The vendors are friendly and eager to show off their wares, and you'll find a dazzling array of colors and textures on display. There are mountains of spices like cumin, sumac, and paprika, as well as exotic blends like baharat and ras el hanout. There are also teas, nuts, dried fruits, and sweets to try.

But the Spice Bazaar is not just a place to buy ingredients for your next meal. It is also a fascinating cultural experience, giving you a glimpse into the history and traditions of Istanbul. The bazaar was originally built as part of the New Mosque complex, and the revenues from the shops were used to support the mosque's upkeep. Today, it is still an important part of the community, with vendors selling everything from soap and ceramics to textiles and souvenirs.

When you visit the Spice Bazaar, be sure to take your time and explore all the nooks and crannies. It can be overwhelming at first, but it's worth the effort to seek out the hidden treasures. You might find a vendor who sells a special blend of tea that becomes your new favorite, or a spice that inspires you to try a new recipe.

Also, don't be afraid to haggle! Bargaining is a time-honored tradition in Istanbul, and the vendors expect it. Just be respectful and polite, and remember that they are trying to make a living.

Finally, be sure to bring your camera. The Spice Bazaar is a feast for the senses, with its colorful displays and bustling crowds. You'll want to capture the memories to share with your friends and family back home.

Overall, the Spice Bazaar is a must-see destination for anyone visiting Istanbul. It's a unique and immersive experience that will leave you with memories that last a lifetime.

The Maiden's Tower: A Historical and Romantic Island Destination in the Bosphorus

The Maiden's Tower, also known as Kiz Kulesi, is a historical and romantic destination in the Bosphorus that offers stunning views of the city of Istanbul. The tower is situated on a small islet near the Asian coast of the Bosphorus, and its origins date back to the Byzantine period.

Legend has it that a sultan was warned by a seer that his daughter would be bitten by a snake and die on her 18th birthday. In an effort to protect her, the sultan built the Maiden's Tower on the islet and kept his daughter there. Unfortunately, the seer's prophecy still came true, and the princess was bitten by a snake that had been brought into the tower inside a basket of fruit. Today, the tower is a popular tourist attraction and can be reached by boat from the European or Asian side of Istanbul.

Visitors to the Maiden's Tower can take in stunning views of the Bosphorus and the city of Istanbul from the tower's observation deck. The tower also features a restaurant and a small museum that showcases the history of the tower and its surrounding area.

In addition to its historical significance and stunning views, the Maiden's Tower is also a popular destination for romantic dinners and events. Couples can enjoy a special dinner or drinks at the tower's restaurant, which offers panoramic views of the city and the Bosphorus.

The Maiden's Tower is a unique and fascinating destination in Istanbul, steeped in both history and romance. This small tower sits on a small islet in the Bosphorus Strait, just off the coast of the city's Asian side. It is surrounded by myths and legends that have been passed down through generations, making it a truly magical place to visit.

The tower has been a part of Istanbul's skyline for centuries, and its origins are shrouded in mystery. It is said to have been built during the Byzantine era, but its true purpose remains unknown. Over the years, the tower has served as a lighthouse, a defensive fortification, and even a quarantine station during times of plague. Today, it is one of Istanbul's most popular tourist attractions, known for its stunning views and romantic atmosphere.

Visitors to the Maiden's Tower can explore its rich history through a variety of exhibits and displays. The tower houses a museum that showcases the history of the Bosphorus

Strait, as well as artifacts and artifacts from the tower itself. The top of the tower offers panoramic views of the city and the sea, providing a unique vantage point for taking in Istanbul's beauty.

One of the most popular ways to experience the Maiden's Tower is to visit it at night. The tower is beautifully lit up after dark, casting a warm and inviting glow across the water. Many visitors choose to enjoy a romantic dinner or a drink at the tower's restaurant, taking in the stunning views while savoring delicious Turkish cuisine.

The Maiden's Tower is also a popular spot for marriage proposals, with its romantic atmosphere and breathtaking views providing the perfect backdrop for a special moment. Many couples choose to visit the tower as part of their honeymoon, making it a truly unforgettable destination.

Whether you are a history buff, a romantic at heart, or simply looking for a unique and memorable experience in Istanbul, the Maiden's Tower is not to be missed. Its beauty and charm will captivate you from the moment you set foot on the island, leaving you with lasting memories of this enchanting destination.

Chora Church: A Guide to Istanbul's Most Beautiful Mosaic and Fresco Art

Chora Church, also known as the Kariye Museum, is one of the most stunning examples of Byzantine art and architecture in Istanbul. Located in the Edirnekapi neighborhood of Istanbul, this church is famous for its breathtaking mosaic and fresco art, which has been beautifully preserved and restored over the centuries.

Originally built in the 5th century, the church underwent major renovations and expansions in the 11th and 12th centuries, during which time most of its impressive mosaics and frescoes were added. The artwork tells the story of the life of Christ and the Virgin Mary, as well as various saints and biblical scenes.

One of the most famous pieces of art at Chora Church is the "Anastasis," a stunning fresco depicting the Resurrection of Christ. The painting is particularly famous for its striking use of color and light, which creates a sense of depth and movement.

Another impressive artwork at Chora Church is the mosaic of the Virgin Mary and Child, which is located in the dome of the church's nave. The mosaic is particularly noteworthy for its use of gold leaf, which creates a shimmering effect in the sunlight that streams through the church's windows.

In addition to its artwork, Chora Church is also known for its impressive architecture. The church features a mix of Byzantine and Ottoman elements, with intricate stonework and ornate decoration both inside and outside the building.

Today, Chora Church is a popular tourist attraction and museum. Visitors can take a guided tour of the church to learn more about its history and artwork, as well as to admire the stunning details and colors of its mosaics and frescoes.

Visiting the Chora Church is a must for anyone who appreciates the beauty of Byzantine art. The church was originally built in the 4th century as part of a monastery, but the current building dates back to the 11th century. The Chora Church is located in the western part of Istanbul and is easily accessible by public transport.

As you approach the church, you'll notice the beautiful exterior brickwork and intricate stone carvings. Once inside, you'll be struck by the magnificence of the mosaic and fresco art that adorns the walls and ceilings. The Chora Church is known for its exquisite depictions of scenes from the life of Jesus Christ, the Virgin Mary, and various saints and martyrs.

One of the most impressive features of the Chora Church is its dome, which is covered in gold mosaics. The mosaic depicts the Ascension of Christ, surrounded by angels and the apostles. The mosaic is particularly impressive when viewed from the ground, where you can appreciate its full beauty.

In addition to the mosaics, the Chora Church is also famous for its frescoes. The frescoes depict scenes from the Old and New Testaments, as well as various saints and martyrs. The frescoes are particularly striking for their use of color and detail, and they offer a unique glimpse into the religious and cultural life of Byzantine Istanbul.

When visiting the Chora Church, be sure to take your time to appreciate the art and architecture. There is a small museum on site that offers additional information about the history of the church and the art that it contains. If you have a particular interest in Byzantine art, the Chora Church is an absolute must-see.

Suleymaniye Mosque: A Visit to Istanbul's Largest and Most Impressive Mosque

Located on a hill overlooking Istanbul's Golden Horn, the Suleymaniye Mosque is one of the city's most iconic landmarks. Commissioned by Sultan Suleiman the Magnificent in the 16th century, the mosque is known for its grand architecture and beautiful design.

History and Architecture:
The Suleymaniye Mosque was designed by the famous Ottoman architect, Mimar Sinan, and completed in 1557. It was built as a tribute to Sultan Suleiman's reign and to symbolize his power and wealth. The mosque is considered to be one of Mimar Sinan's masterpieces, and its design has influenced architecture throughout the world.

The mosque's architecture is a blend of Ottoman and Byzantine styles, with its massive domes, elegant arches, and intricate tile work. The main dome of the mosque is 47 meters high, making it one of the largest in the world. The mosque also features four minarets, which represent the four caliphs of Islam.

Visiting the Mosque:
Visitors to the Suleymaniye Mosque can enter through the courtyard, which is surrounded by a colonnade of domed arches. The courtyard is decorated with beautiful gardens and fountains, making it a peaceful place to relax and take in the view.

Once inside the mosque, visitors can admire the intricate tile work, calligraphy, and beautiful stained glass windows. The main prayer hall is an impressive space, with the giant dome at its center and marble columns lining the walls.

It is important to dress modestly and remove your shoes before entering the mosque. Women are also required to cover their hair.

Nearby Attractions:
The Suleymaniye Mosque is located in the historic district of Istanbul and is surrounded by other important landmarks, including the Grand Bazaar, the Spice Bazaar, and the Galata Tower. Visitors can easily spend a day exploring the area and taking in the history and culture of Istanbul.

In conclusion, the Suleymaniye Mosque is a must-visit destination for anyone traveling to Istanbul. With its grand architecture and rich history, it is a perfect representation of the city's unique blend of cultures and traditions.

Beyoglu District: Exploring Istanbul's Bohemian and Artistic Side

Beyoglu is one of the most vibrant and cultural districts in Istanbul. Situated on the European side of the city, it is a hub for artists, musicians, writers, and bohemian types. This area has been the center of Istanbul's cultural and intellectual life for over a century, and it is still an important destination for both locals and visitors.

History and Culture

Beyoglu's history dates back to the Byzantine Empire, but it began to take on its current identity in the 19th century. During the Ottoman period, the district was home to diplomats, merchants, and foreigners. Later, in the early 20th century, it became a center of art and culture, as well as a popular destination for intellectuals and artists.

Today, the district is still a hub of creative activity, with a range of art galleries, music venues, theaters, and literary cafes. The streets of Beyoglu are lined with colorful buildings that have a distinct European feel, reflecting the influence of the many foreign residents who have called the area home over the years.

Sights and Attractions

Beyoglu is home to many of Istanbul's most famous sights and attractions. The iconic Galata Tower offers stunning panoramic views of the city, while the historic Galata Bridge spans the Golden Horn and connects Beyoglu to the Old City.

One of the most famous streets in Beyoglu is Istiklal Avenue, a long pedestrian thoroughfare that is lined with shops, cafes, and historic buildings. At the end of the avenue is Taksim Square, a busy gathering spot and the site of many important events in modern Turkish history.

Art and Culture

Beyoglu is also known for its vibrant arts and culture scene. The Pera Museum, located in the heart of the district, features a collection of Turkish art from the Ottoman period to the present day, as well as a rotating schedule of temporary exhibitions.

In addition to the many galleries and studios located in the area, Beyoglu is home to several theaters and music venues. The Babylon and Nardis Jazz Club are two of the most popular destinations for live music, while the Istanbul Theater Festival is a highlight of the cultural calendar.

Food and Drink

Beyoglu is known for its diverse food and drink scene, with a range of international and local cuisine on offer. Some of the most popular dishes in the area include meze, grilled meats, and seafood. For a traditional Turkish breakfast, try a simit (a sesame-covered bread ring) and some fresh cheese and olives.

In the evening, Beyoglu comes to life with a range of nightlife options, including rooftop bars, live music venues, and trendy clubs. For a taste of the local scene, head to one of the many small cafes and bars that dot the area.

Conclusion

Beyoglu is a fascinating and unique district that showcases the best of Istanbul's cultural and artistic life. With its rich history, stunning architecture, and lively atmosphere, it is a must-visit destination for anyone visiting the city. Whether you are interested in art, history, or simply soaking up the local culture, there is something for everyone in Beyoglu.

Camlica Hill: A Panoramic View of Istanbul from the Asian Side

Camlica Hill, also known as Camlica Tepesi in Turkish, is one of the highest points in Istanbul, offering stunning panoramic views of the city from the Asian side of the Bosphorus. The hill is divided into two sections, the Big Camlica and the Small Camlica, both of which are popular among locals and tourists alike.

History of Camlica Hill
Camlica Hill has a rich history, dating back to the Ottoman Empire, when the hill was used as a hunting ground for the sultans. During the 19th century, the Ottoman rulers transformed the area into a public park, making it accessible to the public.

Today, Camlica Hill is a popular destination for visitors looking for breathtaking views of the city, as well as a serene escape from the hustle and bustle of Istanbul.

What to Do at Camlica Hill
Camlica Hill offers numerous activities and attractions for visitors of all ages. The most popular activity is simply taking in the stunning panoramic views of Istanbul from the observation decks, which provide a bird's eye view of the Bosphorus Strait and the historic Old City.

Visitors can also explore the many parks, gardens, and trails that wind their way up and around the hill. The Big Camlica, which is the higher of the two hills, is home to a beautiful park with walking paths, picnic areas, and a variety of flora and fauna. The Small Camlica, on the other hand, is more residential in nature, with several mansions and villas that date back to the Ottoman era.

One of the most interesting attractions on Camlica Hill is the Camlica Mosque, which was built in the late 20th century and is one of the largest mosques in Istanbul. The mosque's elegant Ottoman-style architecture, beautiful stained-glass windows, and intricate tile work make it a must-see for any visitor.

Getting to Camlica Hill
Camlica Hill is located on the Asian side of Istanbul, and is easily accessible by public transportation or car. Visitors can take a ferry across the Bosphorus from the European side to the Uskudar district, where they can catch a bus or a taxi to the hill. Alternatively, visitors can take a bus or taxi directly from the European side to Camlica Hill.

Visitors can also choose to hike up the hill for a more adventurous approach. The trails are well-marked and easy to navigate, offering a unique perspective of the city along the way.

Conclusion

Whether you're looking for stunning views of Istanbul, a peaceful escape from the city, or a chance to explore the area's rich history and culture, Camlica Hill is a must-see destination. With its beautiful parks, gardens, trails, and attractions, the hill is a perfect place to spend a day and take in the best of what Istanbul has to offer.

Princes' Islands: A Day Trip to Istanbul's Secluded and Serene Islands

The Princes' Islands, a group of nine small islands located in the Sea of Marmara off the coast of Istanbul, are a popular destination for those seeking a break from the hustle and bustle of the city. The islands are known for their tranquility, lush greenery, and charming houses that date back to the Ottoman era.

The four largest islands are Büyükada (meaning "Big Island"), Heybeliada, Burgazada, and Kınalıada. Visitors can reach the islands by ferry from several points in Istanbul, including Kabataş, Eminönü, and Kadıköy. Once on the islands, visitors can explore by foot, rent a bicycle or horse-drawn carriage, or take a scenic tour by boat.

Büyükada is the most visited island and the only one with motorized vehicles allowed. Visitors can hike or bike to the top of the island for stunning views of the sea and surrounding islands. There are also several historic landmarks on the island, including the Ayia Yorgi Church, which is perched on a hill overlooking the island and dates back to the Byzantine era.

Heybeliada, the second-largest island, is home to several monasteries and churches, including the 19th-century Hagia Triada Greek Orthodox Monastery. The island is known for its peaceful streets and is a popular spot for picnics and swimming.

Burgazada is the third-largest island and is known for its charming fishing village and traditional Ottoman houses. Visitors can explore the narrow streets, visit the island's historic church, and relax on its secluded beaches.

Kınalıada is the smallest of the four largest islands and is known for its rugged coastline and crystal-clear waters. Visitors can swim, sunbathe, and explore the island's pine forests.

Overall, the Princes' Islands offer a unique glimpse into Istanbul's past and present, with its quiet and peaceful atmosphere, charming architecture, and stunning views of the sea. A day trip to these islands is highly recommended for anyone looking to escape the busy city and experience a more relaxed and serene side of Istanbul.

Final Thoughts on Istanbul: Reflections and Recommendations for Your Next Visit.

Istanbul is a city that truly captures the heart and imagination. It is a place where ancient and modern cultures blend together in a beautiful and unique way, creating an unforgettable experience for all who visit. Whether you are interested in history, architecture, culture, cuisine, or simply the beauty of the city, Istanbul has something for everyone.

As you reflect on your visit to Istanbul, there are a few things to keep in mind. First and foremost, Istanbul is a large and bustling city, so be sure to plan your itinerary accordingly. There are so many incredible sights to see that it can be overwhelming, so take your time and don't try to cram everything into one trip.

Another thing to keep in mind is that Istanbul is a city of contrasts. While you will find many beautiful and luxurious places to stay, eat, and shop, you will also encounter poverty, overcrowding, and occasional chaos. It's important to keep an open mind and be respectful of the local culture and customs.

Here are some final recommendations to help you make the most of your visit to Istanbul:

- Visit as many historical sites as you can. Istanbul is a city with a rich and varied history, and there are many sites that reflect this. Be sure to visit the Blue Mosque, Hagia Sophia, Topkapi Palace, Chora Church, Suleymaniye Mosque, and other historical landmarks.

- Explore the city's diverse neighborhoods. Each neighborhood in Istanbul has its own unique character and charm. Be sure to explore areas like Sultanahmet, Beyoglu, and Kadikoy, and experience the different cultures and lifestyles within the city.

- Try the local cuisine. Turkish cuisine is delicious and diverse, and you'll find many amazing dishes in Istanbul. Be sure to try kebabs, meze, baklava, and other Turkish delicacies.

- Take a boat tour of the Bosphorus. The Bosphorus is a beautiful and important waterway that separates Europe from Asia. Taking a boat tour of the Bosphorus is a great way to see the city from a different perspective and enjoy some beautiful views.

- Shop at the Grand Bazaar and Spice Bazaar. Istanbul is known for its shopping, and the Grand Bazaar and Spice Bazaar are two of the most famous shopping destinations in the city. Be sure to haggle for a good price and pick up some unique souvenirs.

- Take a day trip to the Princes' Islands. If you're looking for a break from the hustle and bustle of the city, the Princes' Islands are a great destination. These car-free islands are a peaceful retreat, with beautiful views and great seafood.

In conclusion, Istanbul is a city that truly has something for everyone. It's a place that will capture your heart and leave you with memories to last a lifetime. By following these recommendations, you'll be sure to have an unforgettable experience in one of the most beautiful and unique cities in the world.

Printed in Great Britain
by Amazon